j
598.2
Bo   Bosiger, E.
          A bird is born, by E. Bosiger and J. M.
        Guilcher.   Photographs by E. Hosking and R. H.
        Noailles.   N.Y., Sterling, [1963]
          95p.   illus.,photos.   (Sterling nature series)

11,528

          1.Birds.   2.Guilcher, Jean Michael, 1914- ,
        jt.auth.   II.Title.

A
BIRD
IS
BORN

BY
E. BOSIGER AND J.-M. GUILCHER

PHOTOGRAPHS BY
E. HOSKING AND R.-H. NOAILLES

STERLING
PUBLISHING CO., INC. NEW YORK
Oak Tree Press Co., Ltd.
London & Sydney

STERLING NATURE SERIES

Ninth Printing, 1974

Revised Edition, 1963

Sterling Publishing Co., Inc.
419 Park Avenue South, New York, N.Y. 10016
British edition published by Oak Tree Press Co., Ltd., Nassau, Bahamas
Distributed in Australia and New Zealand by Oak Tree Press Co., Ltd.,
P.O. Box J34, Brickfield Hill, Sydney 2000, N.S.W.
Distributed in the United Kingdom and elsewhere in the British Commonwealth
by Ward Lock Ltd., 116 Baker Street, London W 1

Sterling ISBN 0–8069–3504–9 Trade   Oak Tree 7061–2274 7
3505–7 Library

CONTENTS

I. THE BIRTH OF A BIRD

FROM THE TIME a baby bird emerges from the egg to the day it leaves its parents, there is a period of only a few weeks — or at most, a few months. That time represents the bird's childhood — a period as varied as the birds themselves and their surroundings. The strength or weakness of the young birds and the care and training they receive from their parents differ according to the species of bird.

But one feature varies very little — the beginning of life and the amazing development which takes place unseen within the secret covering of the egg. At the outset, the life of the egg is contained in a tiny whitish spot, thousandths of an inch in thickness: this is the nucleus. Ten to thirty days later, a complex living creature fills the shell. This marvelous transformation of the nuclear germ is produced by the gentle warmth transmitted to the eggs by the brooding mother bird.

The first section of this book shows this transformation by following the growth of a chicken's embryo from laying to hatching. The second part then gives an idea of the different kinds of bird growth after birth.

Illus. 1 and 2. These two photographs, taken through the transparent mass of the albumen (the white part of the egg) show two successive stages of the egg at the start of incubation (when the mother hen sits on her brood).

At first the nucleus germ is no more than a tiny dot on the surface of the yolk (called the vitellus). As soon as incubation starts, the germ begins to grow. It becomes a germinal disc (see Illus. 1), then a living membrane (skin-like tissue). It rapidly extends over the surface of the yolk. (See Illus. 2.) Within 48 hours, the membrane almost reaches the center of the yolk; at the end of the fourth day, it covers the entire yolk and seals it. The yolk is by then enclosed in a living skin — the yolk sac.

Only the very center of the germinal disc is destined to form the chicken. This is called the embryo. The yolk sac is used mainly to feed the embryo. It has a secretion which turns the yolk into a liquid food which is rich in nourishment. The yolk sac digests it and passes it on to the embryo.

INTERNAL VIEW OF THE EGG:

1. (Upper photo) After 12 hours of incubation.
2. (Lower photo) After 24 hours of incubation.

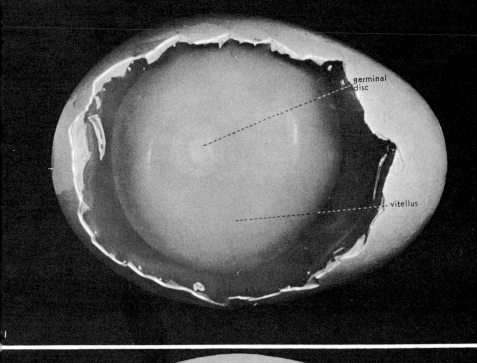

germinal
disc

vitellus

1

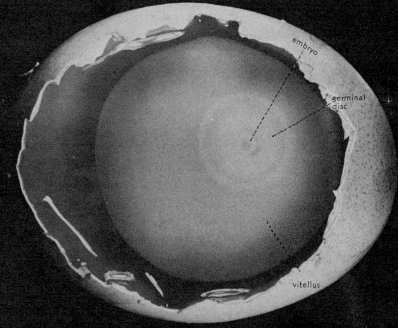

embryo

germinal
disc

vitellus

2

Illus. 3. This photograph taken through the albumen after the second day shows that the yolk sac has already developed greatly. The albumen conceals the yellow yolk, which is partly turned into liquid and sagging, and has already lost its spherical shape.

The most noticeable feature is a circular network of blood vessels which is beginning to appear on the yolk sac. A comparison of Illus. 3 and 4, which were taken at an interval of 12 hours, gives some idea of the speed of growth. In time the network will cover the entire sac.

The embryo occupies the center of the network. Illus. 5 shows it all on a larger scale. Notice the grayish outline with the large head and slender body. All the large blood vessels radiate from the body. To the right and left a fan-shaped pattern of arteries carries blood out from the embryo to the exterior. As the arteries pass through the tissues which absorb the liquefied and digested yolk, the blood becomes filled with the digested materials. Large collector veins on the outer edges of the network receive the blood and return it, enriched by nutritive substances, to the embryo. The whole network forms a drainage system which supplies the embryo with the materials necessary for its growth.

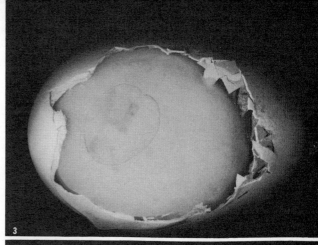

3. After 2½ days
of incubation.

4. After 3 days.

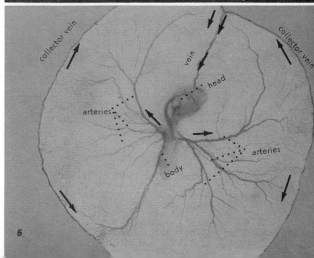

5. Embryo at center
of network of
blood vessels (3½ days).

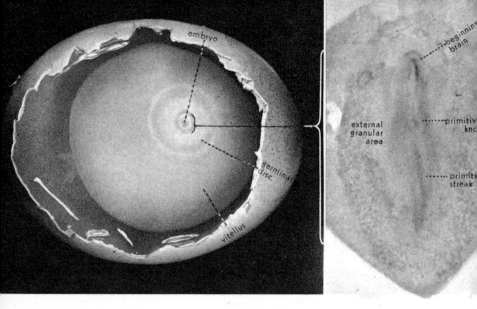

embryo

germinal disc

vitellus

beginning brain

external granular area

primitiv kno

primiti streak

6. Embryo at 19 hours . . .

The primitive knot and the primitive streak shown on the photos play an important role in the development of tissues of the embryo, but they are too complex to discuss in this book.

In order to observe the embryo in these first days of development, and not merely the disc which surrounds it, a microscope is needed. Illustrations 6 to 21 (enlarged about 14 times) show the central zone of the germinal disc and the embryo forming within. The photographs show how the embryo evolves from the first hours of incubation to the fourth day. All the photographs are taken from the same angle — the head of the embryo facing toward the top of the page.

On the first day (Illus. 6), a groove-like depression appears in the area which will later become the head. This tiny wrinkle, barely visible on the surface of the nucleus, is the first hint of the brain that will soon develop. From now on, the changes continue with surprising speed.

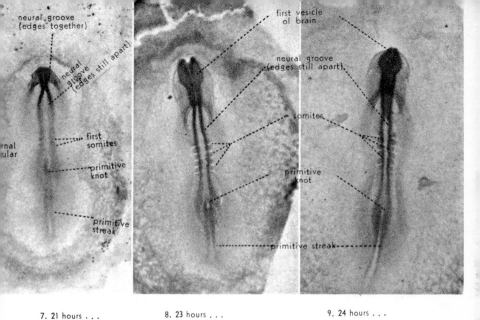

neural groove
(edges together)

neural groove
(edges still apart)

first vesicle
of brain

neural groove
(edges still apart)

somites

nal
ular

first
somites

primitive
knot

primitive
streak

primitive
knot

primitive streak

7. 21 hours . . .   8. 23 hours . . .   9. 24 hours . . .

In the hours and days following, the depression gradually extends to the other end of the body. It becomes deeper. Its edges grow closer together, then curve toward each other and meet. The groove begins to close into a tube (Illus. 7 and the following photos). Before the groove is completely closed, the front part of the tube expands to form a large vesicle (a bladder-like cavity within the tissues), shown in Illus. 8, 9, and 10. Then three other vesicles, each smaller than the one before, are formed (11 and 12).

From that moment, the central nervous system is sketched out — the four vesicles correspond to the future brain, the rest of the embryo corresponds to the spinal cord. The second day has hardly begun.

11

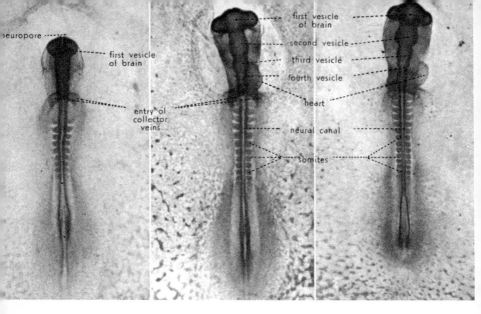

neuropore

first vesicle of brain

entry of collector veins

first vesicle of brain

second vesicle

third vesicle

fourth vesicle

heart

neural canal

somites

10. 26 hours . . .   11. 30 hours . . .   12. 32 hours . . .

Meanwhile, on a deeper level, the blood circulation system is being developed. The organs that we have seen show through the transparent surface tissues. The embryo is surrounded by a granular area (Illus. 6, 7, 8). Here, in this area, the blood corpuscles will be produced long before the embryo can make its own blood. Here, and in the embryo, will appear the blood vessels which form the first elements in the drainage system shown in Illus. 5. In Illus. 10, we can already make out the base of two large veins behind the head. The blood will soon flow from the outside of the yolk through these veins. Soon afterward, the heart itself takes shape in front of the junction where the veins meet (Illus. 11 and 12) and begins to beat within this creature which still barely exists.

12

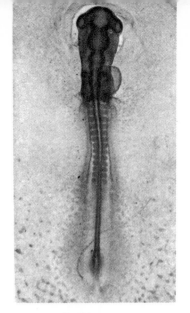

13. 36 hours . . .

Through the transparent tissues, we can also see a series of small dark spots steadily becoming more numerous. Called somites, these are lined up in pairs along the length of the trunk. They will later develop, in a complex way, into various organs — muscles, bone skeleton, kidneys and so on.

One of the important features of the next few hours in the egg is the appearance of a protective covering. In Illus. 13, we can see a gray band just beginning to appear in front of the embryo, enclosing the front part of the head. It is a fold of delicate skin which will grow very quickly, and extend to form a hood over the head and along the embryo's sides. The fold will gradually spread over the surface of the entire body, the hood will continue to extend backward, and a transparent tunnel will cover the embryo from head to tail. This covering membrane is called the amnion.

13

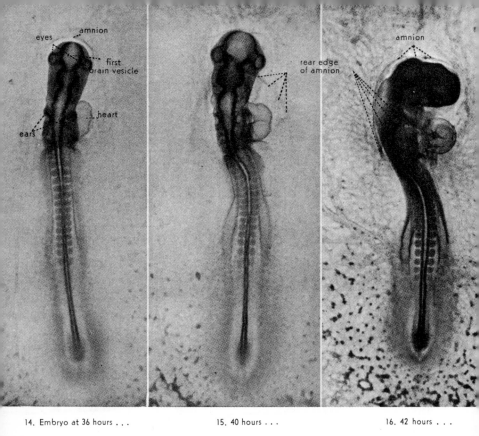

eyes
amnion
first
brain vesicle
heart
ears

rear edge
of amnion

amnion

14. Embryo at 36 hours . . .   15. 40 hours . . .   16. 42 hours . . .

Illus. 14 to 20 show several stages in the amnion's growth. In the first of these photographs, the amnion is no more than a crease of skin which can barely be seen in front of the brain. In Illus. 15, it already overlaps the first vesicle and part of the second. Because of its transparency the amnion is hard to see clearly, but the edge of its open end gaping toward the rear is already in view. In later stages, it becomes more clearly visible. It covers the whole head (16), extends further and further back (17 and 18), until it finally covers the entire body (19 and 20). For some time, there remains a circular opening

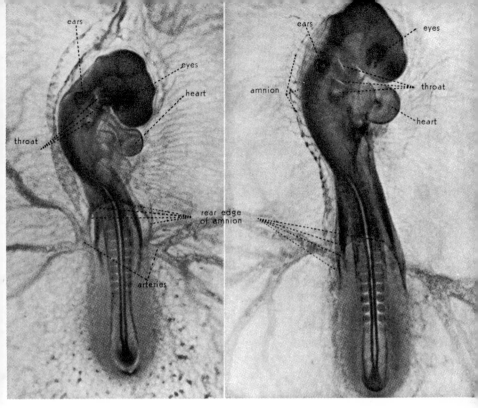

17. 46 hours . . .   18. 54 hours . . .

near the tail (19). It grows narrower and then
closes completely. The embryo is now enclosed in
a sealed cavity, which rapidly fills with liquid secreted
from the containing walls. The embryo, bathed in
this amniotic fluid, is now in an environment suitable
for its further development. This watery bed cushions
the embryo against shock from the outside and
protects its delicate tissues from drying up.

The embryo takes on firmer outlines and its
general shape becomes clearer. In Illus. 14, it was
still part of the tissues of the yolk sac. In Illus. 20,

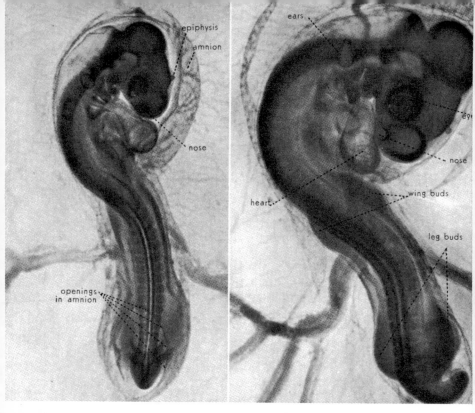

19. 62 hours . . .   20. 4 days

it is entirely separate, joined to these tissues only
by an umbilical cord (not seen in the photo). As
the embryo begins to emerge as a separate entity,
it turns on its left side. The movement affects the
head first, then gradually spreads throughout the
body.

The circulatory system and the nervous system
develop. The sense organs (eyes, ears, nose, throat)
begin to establish themselves. Illus. 20 also shows
the swellings (buds) which will eventually grow into
wings and legs.

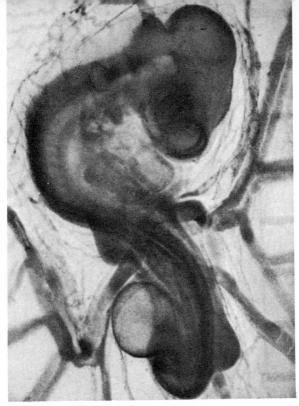

21. 4 days

Illus. 21. In this photograph, taken at the same
stage as Illus. 20, a transparent bubble is visible at
the rear of the body. It is an extension of the intestine,
which has broken through (ruptured) the amnion.
Emerging from the lower surface of the embryo, it
turns sideways and passes below the bud of the left
leg. This is the birth of an important organ — the
allantois. As it develops, it will grow larger. Going
around all obstacles, it will occupy all the available
space, surrounding the white of the egg, lying against
the shell. It will take up more and more room as
the yolk and albumen of the egg decrease.

The allantois performs several important functions in the life of the embryo. In the first place, it is a respiratory organ, through which the embryo breathes. Since the egg shell is porous and the outer wall of the allantois which adheres to the shell is covered by a network of blood vessels, the blood can come into contact with the air. The mother hen turns her eggs over regularly, thus aiding ventilation on all sides. The collector veins of the allantois bring oxygen to the embryo (just as those of the yolk sac carry back nourishment). The allantois' veins also supply the embryo with water collected from the white of the egg. Finally, the embryo's urine is voided into the cavity of the allantois where it accumulates in the form of crystals.

Illus. 22 and 23. These two pictures show embryos of four and a half days and of six days. They are now big enough to be examined through a magnifying glass rather than a microscope.

The embryo is lying on its left side in the center of the blood network which nourishes it. From the fourth to sixth day, it has greatly increased in size. The head is enormous, the body is very small. A lens has appeared in the huge eye. The buds that will become limbs are growing longer.

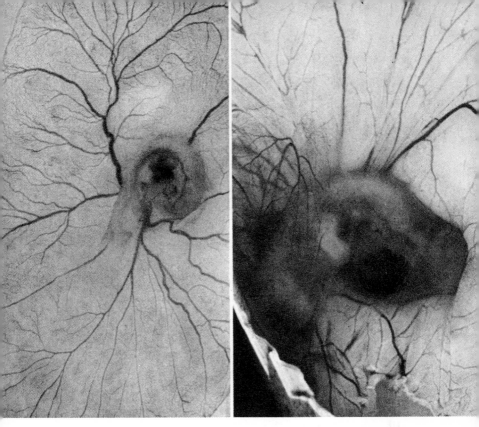

22. Embryo at 4½ days.   23. Embryo at 6 days.

The allantois is also growing rapidly. Its transparency makes it hard to see, but Illus. 23 gives us an idea of its general shape if we follow the course of a blood vessel contained in the allantois wall. It arises on the left side of the embryo, curves and then appears below the right side. If we look carefully we can see the edge of the allantois itself.

The embryo is now almost an inch long—the rest of its development can be followed with the naked eye. Illus. 24 to 30 are only slightly enlarged. The allantois has been withdrawn from most of these eggs since it has grown quite large and would hide the embryo. In Illus. 25, a fragment remains near the bottom of the left side of the shell.

The embryo is now beginning to look like a young bird. The mouth opening has appeared; the beak is formed (24). The eye is wide open in the amniotic liquid — we can clearly see the pupil (25). Behind the eye is the ear opening. The wings and legs, no longer the shapeless stumps of the earlier stage, are easily recognizable. In Illus. 24, note the network of blood vessels developed on the yolk sac. Note, too, between the legs, the umbilical cord connecting the yolk sac to the embryo.

On the skin there has appeared a regular pattern of tiny pores (25). From each one will emerge a very tiny feather of down.

The food reserves of the yolk are diminishing. As the yolk sac begins to sag, the embryo takes up more and more room.

24. (Above) Internal view of egg at 9 days.

25. (Below) Internal view of egg at 10 days.

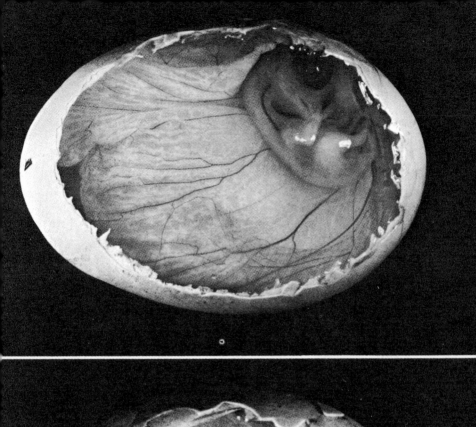

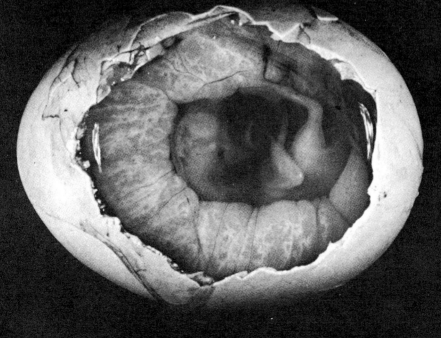

Illus. 26 and 27. On the 12th day, the embryo is still bare. Only a few feathers have appeared on the tiny pores. By the 16th day, the whole body is covered with down, which is already long and sticks together in damp wisps. On the 12th day, the embryo has plenty of room within the shell. But by the 16th day, it is so cramped for space that it must lie huddled against the wall of the shell. The sac — its food reserves diminished — is crushed into the other end of the egg.

The body has grown more than the head. The eye, formerly wide open in the amniotic fluid, closes. It will not open again till the hatching.

The underside of the beak has an angular projection — the egg-tooth. It can be seen in Illus. 26, but it is more developed in the following stage (27). It is with this diamond-shaped tooth that the chicken will pierce the shell.

In Illus. 26, the toes and claws are already formed.

26. (Above) Internal view of egg at 12 days.

27. (Below) Internal view of egg at 16 days.

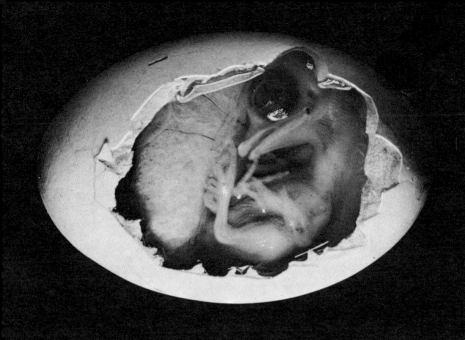

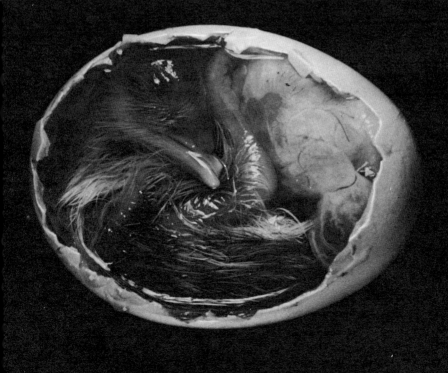

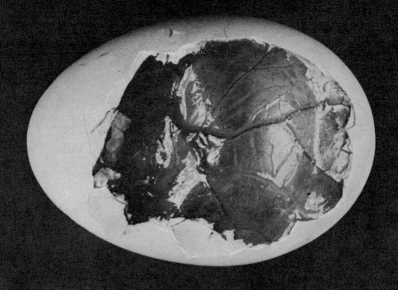

28

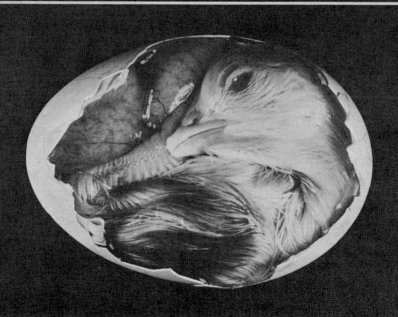

29

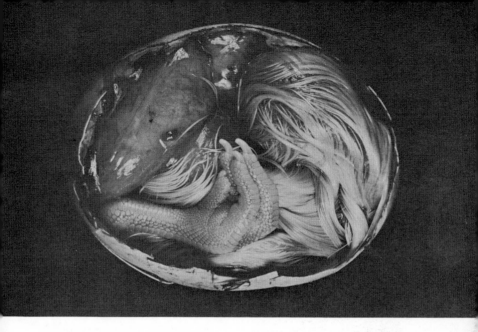

28. (Above, left page) Allantois at 18 days.

29. (Below) The chicken at 18 days.

30. (Above, this page) The leg at 20 days.

If we carefully remove the shell from an 18-day-old egg (Illus. 28), we discover the wall of the allantois still adhering to it. Removing the allantois, an almost complete and fully proportioned chicken is revealed (Illus. 29). Molded against the shell, it seems to be sleeping peacefully. The growth of the embryo is nearly complete. The powerful leg (Illus. 30) is now ready to support the little bird which is about to be born.

On about the 20th day, the chicken, having reached its full term of development, awakens in the egg and breaks the amnion which has been enclosing it. The attentive mother hen can hear its muffled peeping.

It is not till the 21st day that the chicken tries to break out of the shell. The shell has become thinner — part of its chalky content was used in the growth of the chicken's skeleton. But it is still not easy for the new chicken, with its untried muscles, to break the shell. It begins applying its egg-tooth against the wall of the shell until it makes a small star-shaped hole. After a pause for rest, it makes a second hole near the first one — then a third, a fourth and so on until the shell is cracked and a panel is cut out of it (Illus. 31).

Then, pressing its head against the panel, the chicken gathers all its strength in a tremendous effort to be born. It pushes the shell apart and emerges (Illus. 32).

31 and 32. The twenty-first day.

Illus. 33. The egg is open. The chicken pulls itself all the way

out of the broken shell and collapses, exhausted (Illus. 34).

After 15 minutes' rest, it raises its head, pulls itself up and

squats on its legs and tail (Illus. 35 and 36).

37

38

Soon, the newborn bird stands up and shakes itself. Its damp down is quickly dried under the wings of the mother hen. An hour later (Illus. 39), it is a fluffy bundle of down, with sparkling eyes, already firmly on its legs.

By tomorrow, along with its brothers and sisters, the chick will parade behind its mother, running up to her when she clucks, scrambling for the ear of grain she lets fall. In the beginning, the baby chickens will only peck at the food she presents to them. Later on they will find their own nourishment. It is almost the only lesson which nature has left them to learn.

2. HOW BIRDS GROW

ALL KINDS of birds have eggs and embryos that pass through the same basic stages. In all of them the same organs appear in the same order. All have a yolk sac, an amnion, an allantois. Although one kind of bird differs from another, the differences are only matters of detail — how big the different organs grow, when the feathers appear and so forth. These differences begin to show up most clearly during the last stages of the embryo's growth.

Some birds are born vigorous and active, like the young chicken. Little ducklings can swim and frolic in the water when they are only two days old. Several hours after breaking their shell, young curlews are scurrying behind their parents. It is the same with partridges, quail, seagulls, lapwings, swans, pheasants and others. For them, the nest is merely the place where they hatch. The young birds' education begins immediately after they leave the nest.

The lessons they have to learn are simple ones. They must learn to grasp food with their beaks, to find food for themselves and to run to the mother when called. Within a week, the main lessons have been learned and the young birds have achieved a degree of independence. But independence will not be complete until that still distant day when the birds' wings are strong enough for flight.

The childhood of a sparrow, a tomtit or a woodpecker is very different. In these species, the young birds are born blind and helpless. Their skin is naked, their limbs are powerless. It is almost as if they had broken through their shells too soon. Because of this, they are not ready to learn anything yet. It is up to their parents to give them warmth, to provide them with food and to keep them clean. It is a task from which there is no rest.

The young birds remain in the nest, totally dependent on those nursing them. They do not leave the protection of their cradle until their bodies are covered with feathers and their new wings are capable of flight. Only then do their parents begin to teach them and gradually make them completely independent.

We will use the curlew and the tomtit as examples of opposite kinds of development — that of a bird independent right after birth and one that is helpless. The owl will show a type that is in between the two.

3. THE CURLEW

T HE CURLEW is a bird that is common along the coasts of Europe. It can reach a length of two feet from the tip of its beak to the end of its tail, and it can weigh up to two pounds. It is an excellent flyer, capable of covering long distances.

During the summer it nests in the north or the east of Europe; it spends the winter in Africa or in India. Some curlews, however, do settle in Europe for the winter and may even remain to nest there in the spring.

They live by the seashore or the mouth of a river or lake. With their long curved beaks, they rummage in the seaweed and the mud to find the worms and shellfish they feed on. They nest on the ground in the high grasses of the sand dunes, marshes or damp meadows.

The pair shown in Illus. 1 have made their nest in a marsh. The male and female take turns sitting on the eggs. The two are so alike that it is impossible

1.

to tell whether male or female is sitting on the eggs
in the picture. When they remain motionless, their
flecked plumage makes them practically invisible.
Because of this protective coloration, the eggs and
the newly hatched birds are kept safe from enemies.

2.

Illus. 2. One of the curlews (notice the long legs) is preparing to sit on the eggs. The nest is a simple hollow in the earth, furnished with a few scraps of brushwood. It contains four large eggs which are olive-colored, speckled with brown. Incubation will begin only after the fourth egg has been laid.

3.

Illus. 3. Here the bird is on the nest with its legs folded under it and its beak tucked into its back feathers. This is the position for sleeping.

The birds sit for 26 to 30 days, relieving each other at intervals.

4. (Above)

5. (Below)

Illus. 4. Since the incubation of the four eggs began at the same time, they hatch almost at the same time too. Note that their shape is more pointed than hens' eggs.

Illus. 5. Two little curlews have just broken out of their shells and lie damp and exhausted from the effort. Their beaks are straight and long already. The egg-tooth can be seen in the one in the background.

Like the hen, the mother curlew warms her newly-born chicks under her feathers. As soon as the little ones are dry, they show their little heads, then their bodies with mottled coats of down (Illus. 6). They can hardly stay in one place. Already, their wide-open eyes are exploring their surroundings. The liveliest of the four ventures out into the grass, the others following. Accompanied by their mother, they leave the nest forever (Illus 7).

At the very outset of their wandering life, the young curlews, like young chickens, learn to feed themselves. At first the parents put food in front of them. Then, after two to four days, the little ones find it themselves.

From birth, their thick down keeps them warm. However, when the weather becomes cold, they take shelter under their mother's wings. As their feathers grow, they become more independent.

7.

6.

But until they can fly away they will need protection. Their natural camouflage is not enough to defend them against their enemies — marauders of the grass and air. One of the parent birds always remains on guard nearby.

After 33 to 35 days, the young birds, like adults in all but size, will be able to fly. For one last week, the parents will guide them in their new life. Then it will be time for parting. Not until they are about three months old will the young curlews reach their full size.

4. THE TOMTIT

O<small>F THE MANY SPECIES</small> of tits, the tomtit (or great tit) is the most common in France. It lives in woods and gardens, feeding on insects, berries and seeds. Because the tomtit destroys so many insects, it is of great service to man. When the cold weather comes, the tomtits do not leave for other lands. Gathering in small bands, they are joined by other tits and sometimes other birds, such as wrens. The tomtits lead the group from tree to tree in search of the food which has now become so scarce. The bands break up before the end of winter, and in February, the tits, who are early nesters, pair off in search of a place for their nests. They must have a sheltered and hidden place — a deep hole in a tree, a crack in a wall (Illus. 1). They nest readily in artificial nesting boxes, such as those pictured in Illus. 2 and 3. Usually, however, as soon as they have found a site, they begin to build their own nest.

←1.

2. Closed nesting box.

3. Open nesting box.

In contrast to the haphazard nest of the curlew, the cup-shaped nest of the tomtit is fashioned with skill (Illus. 4 and 5). The outside is made of coarse materials — twigs and bits of straw. Then there is a thick layer of grass and moss. Finally, the interior is of soft insulating materials — feathers, rabbit fur, horsehair, cotton and wool.

The mother lays from 6 to 14 eggs (there are 9 in the photograph). They are white, speckled with gray and rust. Only she sits on them. The young ones are born after 13 or 14 days (Illus. 5).

4. (Opposite page, above) The nest and the eggs.

5. (Opposite page, below) The newborn tomtits.

6. The young tomtit after leaving the shell.

Illus. 6. Compared with the newborn chicks of the hen or the curlew, the young tomtit is a pitiful object. Its head is enormous, its body unformed. Its undeveloped limbs have no strength, and its eyes and ears are closed. Except for a few tufts of down on head and back, the skin is bare, reddish and wrinkled. Without the warmth of the nest and the shelter and added warmth of the mother's body, the young tits would soon die of cold. For 8 or 10 days they cannot do without their mother's care.

Nor can they feed themselves unaided. They can only raise their heads and open their beaks to beg for food. The soft bright yellow rim on their beaks gives the gaping mouth a large circular outline. (Illus. 8).

7.-8. Newborn tomtits on the day of hatching.

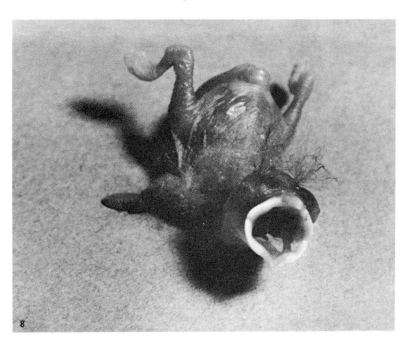

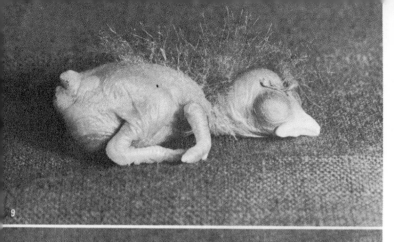

9. First day

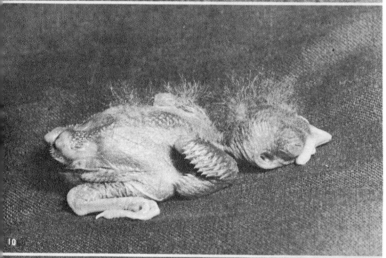

10. Fourth day

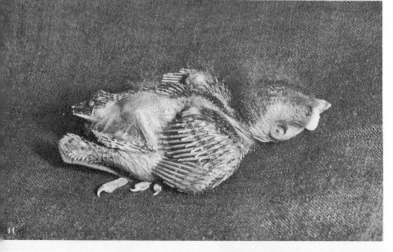

11. Eighth day

12. Tenth day

13. Fourteenth day

14. Eighteenth day

While the creature that emerges from the egg is almost in a larval state (resembling a wingless, immature insect), it is a lively and well-feathered young tit when it leaves the nest. Illus. 9-14 show the surprising transformation.

At first glance, we notice the remarkable change in the young bird's posture. During the first 8 days (Illus. 9-11) it lies prostrate, its head on the ground. After the 10th day (Illus. 12-14), it can use its legs to lift its body and head.

By the 8th day (Illus. 11), the rapid growth of the body has changed all the proportions of the bird. The organs of digestion — stomach, intestine, liver — have grown larger. At the same time, the yellow pad on the beak has stretched along the sides of the mouth. The wings and legs are taking shape. The plumage is developing on the head, the back, the wings and the tail. The feather sheaths emerge from the skin (Illus. 10) and get longer (Illus. 11). Soon, the feathers themselves grow out of the sheaths and gradually become larger (Illus. 12, 13, 14). But even in the last stage, a few wisps of thin baby down may be seen among the adult plumage.

The eyes do not open until about the 9th day. (The bird shown in Illus. 12 is able to open his eyes.) By the 18th day (Illus. 14), the young tit differs from the adults only in the less vivid hues of its plumage.

15.   16.

While remaining in the nest, the young ones do nothing but sleep and eat. Those shown in Illus. 15 and 16 are 10 days old. Their eyes are open. All can raise themselves on their legs (Illus. 16). Each bird is slightly different from his brothers. (Compare the plumage of the bird in the foreground in Illus. 16 with the one on the extreme right.)

As soon as they hear their parents, they sit up (Illus. 16) with their necks stretched and trembling, their beaks open, chirping loudly in expectation of a meal.

17.   18.

All day long the parents are busy flying to and
fro between the hunting grounds and the nest. It has
been observed that the parents make up to 390
journeys each day to feed their young. In Illus. 17, it
is the father that is perched on the side of the nesting
box. The baby birds still cannot grasp the food he
brings. He must force it down into the beaks stretched
toward him (Illus. 18). The bright coloring of the
mouth and beak rim guide him in the semi-darkness.

The nest is always kept clean — droppings of the
little ones are covered with a jelly-like mucus, and
are picked up and thrown away by the tidy parents
(Illus. 19).

19.→

After a period of between 17 and 21 days, the young birds, who are now like the adults, leave the nest at last. Their wings are strong, and they soon learn to flit from branch to branch. Their plumage is thick and feathers cover the whole body. They no longer need the protective warmth of the nest.

They still do not know how to eat by themselves, and the parents must continue to feed them. They must also be protected from the dangers menacing them — the prowling cat, the sparrow-hawk gliding overhead, the dormouse which lurks among the branches at night. The birds' babyhood, especially the weeks that follow emergence from the nest, is a time of great danger. Observations made over many years have shown that 87 per cent of the young tits die before the following spring. The only way these totally inexperienced youngsters can stay alive is to remain in contact with their parents. For that reason, they follow the older birds everywhere, guided by the calls made by the mother and father as they move about.

In the course of this wandering family life, the young learn to grasp food in their beaks, to scan the branches, leaves and buds for the gnats, eggs and insect larvae which are hidden there. As a rule, they can feed themselves by the time they are a month old. That is the age of the little tit shown in Illus. 20. The

20.

yellow beak rim is already so reduced that it can barely be seen. It will eventually disappear completely.

After two to four weeks of life away from the nest, parental care ends. The young tits are now fully grown and their education is complete. From now on they will be self-sufficient. And before the summer, the parents will have reared a second brood.

5. THE LITTLE OWL

T HE LITTLE OWL is one of the commonest night birds. It spends the entire year in the same place. Males and females are alike in size and appearance. (They are about 8 to 10 inches from beak to tail.) The female has a slightly darker face.

The owl has only one brood a year — toward the end of April or the beginning of May. Like the tomtit, it likes to nest in a deep hole in a tree or wall or in an abandoned burrow. But this bird need not take any building material there, for it builds no nest. Its four or five eggs lie on the bottom of the hole. The female sits on them for 28 days.

The owl in the picture (Illus. 1) is established in a rabbit's hole. Her little ones have just hatched, and she is going out to hunt for food. The camera's flash has caught her on the threshold of her burrow, just as she was opening her wings.

←1.

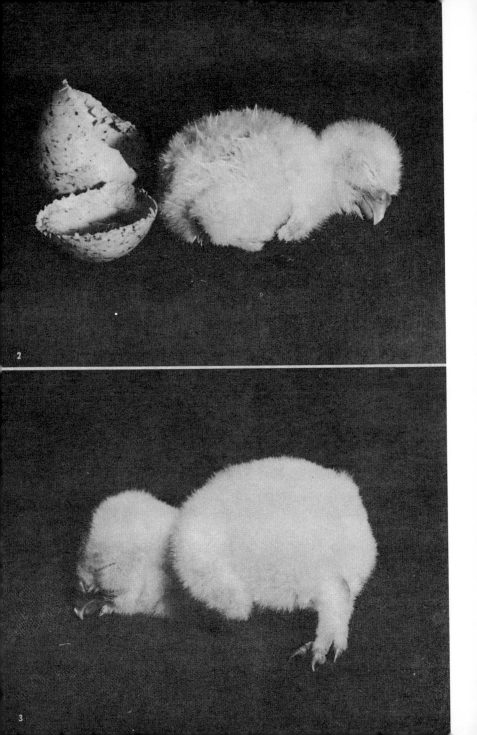

2

3

In Illus. 2-6 we see one of the newborn owls. Like the young chicken or the curlew, it is covered with a thick coat of down and does not need any external warmth. Like the baby tit, its eyes are closed — not to open until about the 10th day.

Unable to walk, it crawls on its stomach, pushing with its legs (Illus. 3). The legs have broad horny heels and strong claws (Illus. 5). The curved beak is also powerful (Illus. 6). With the aid of the beak and claws, the blind young owl can tear at the prey which his mother brings him.

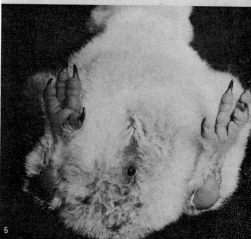

7.

The mother owl cares little about the condition of her nest, where droppings and rubbish accumulate. But she feeds her children well, giving them anything edible that comes her way — a beetle flying in the twilight (Illus. 7), an earthworm attracted to the surface by the coolness of the night (Illus. 8), and larger game like a mole or a mouse (Illus. 9).

8.→

10.

In Illus. 10 we see that the young owl, now a month old, is beginning to resemble the adults. This is the first time it has left the burrow; it ventures no farther than the threshold.

Within a few days, its wings will be strong enough for flight. Then it will leave its underground hole, and begin its apprenticeship as a nighttime hunter under the guidance of its mother.

Female Shrike

6. NEST-DWELLERS AND NEST-LEAVERS

BIRDS WHO LEAVE the nest early, like the curlew and the chicken, are called "nest-leavers." Extreme in this sense are the mound birds of Australia and Malaya. They abandon their eggs on the beach or in the moist earth of the forest. There the eggs are hatched by the heat of the sun or the warmth brought by decaying vegetable matter. The birds are born with full plumage. They never know their parents, and are self-sufficient from the start.

Other birds, like the tit, are quite helpless when they are born, and belong to the "nest-dwelling" group. Most songbirds of the woods and gardens are of this type.

But between the "nest-dwellers" and the "nest-leavers" there are many in-between types. Within each group, too, the kinds of behavior are quite different. No species of bird is exactly like any other. Here, as everywhere, nature shows her variety of ways and uses many methods to make sure that all species survive. In this chapter, we will have some examples.

Black-Headed Gull

The black-headed gull nests in colonies on the edge of ponds, in dunes by the sea and on sandy islets. The nest, usually built close to the water's edge, is made of twigs, reeds and rushes piled together. It contains two to four eggs.

In this respect the gull, like the curlew, differs from most other "nest-leavers," who have a large number of eggs.

The chicks are born after 22 to 24 days of incubation. They leave the nest some days later; until then their parents bring them small insects — winged ants, mosquitoes, sandflies and so on. The baby birds can walk, run and swim at once. They fly at about.the age of five or six weeks. Soon afterward, their parents abandon them.

The bittern is a large wading bird of the heron family, measuring about 28 inches and weighing between 2 and 3 pounds. It likes slow-flowing rivers, marshes, and ponds in which there are reeds. In the daytime, it remains squatting between the stalks. At nightfall, it heads for open water to fish. An excellent diver, it captures fish, frogs and newts, and also eats worms, leeches, shellfish and water insects.

In April it builds its nest in the heart of the forest of reeds. The nest is a thick raft of stems and dry leaves (see Illus. 1). Reeds broken off at water level, but still rooted, make a solid foundation. The female lays five or six large eggs, which she sits on for about 25 days.

The young bitterns are covered with thick rust-colored down. Their eyes and ears are fully open at birth. But they do not leave the nest. The mother brings them food (Illus. 2), and protects them. At the least alarm, she sits erect, with her neck fully stretched, head held high and beak pointed upward. In this position she remains absolutely still (Illus. 3), so that it is difficult to see her in the mass of reeds.

Illus. 4 shows her throwing the remains of the shell off the nest, shortly after hatching her eggs.

The young birds eat only what their mother brings them. Their stay in the nest lasts about two weeks. Then they begin to leave it, but return after each outing.

Only after a month do they abandon the nest completely. For another month they remain hidden in the marsh. At last, their wings are strong enough, and they leave forever.

4.

Heron

The heron is a cousin of the bittern, but its habits are different. It builds its nest — a large platform of branches with raised edges — in the top of a tree. The four or five downy baby birds are lively, but weak on their legs. They spend from five to seven weeks in the nest, eating only what their parents bring them (Illus. 2). When they are about two months old, they are ready to accompany the adult birds, and leave the nest for good.

2.

In April, when the swallow returns from the warm area where it has spent the winter, it hastens to build its nest or to repair the one left the year before. With moist earth mixed with straw, it makes a deep cup which is firmly placed in the angle of a window, under the eaves or in a barn. The interior is lined with grass and feathers. The female lays from four to six eggs.

←Swallow

3.

After 15 days of incubation, the babies come into the world, as naked and powerless as those of the tit. The swallow parents, hunting as they fly, capture a great many insects — flies, mosquitoes, weevils,

4.

winged ants, butterflies and so on. These they feed to
the youngsters (Illus. 3 and 4), by forcing them down
the babies' throats. The young swallows begin to fly
after three weeks.

Hardly bigger than a sparrow, the shrike feeds chiefly on the larger insects — grasshoppers, cockchafers, crickets. The shrike stores its catch for future use by spiking the insects on the thorns of bushes. It is also a great enemy of finches, wrens, linnets and other birds, which it kills and devours.

It nests in thorn hedges and bramble thickets. Its young ones (usually five or six) are born in May or June. During the first days of their life the mother scarcely leaves them. She stays on the nest to keep them warm. The father does most of the hunting. The picture here shows him giving the mother a caterpillar, which she will thrust into the beak of one of the young birds. The male is recognized by the black band which goes from his forehead across his eyes to his neck.

The young shrike develops more rapidly than the young swallow — when it is about 15 days old, it is ready to fly.

Shrike→

Blackbird

The blackbird is commonly seen in the woods and gardens. It feeds on insects, worms, fruits and seeds. Its nest, made of moss and grass plastered together with earth, is built fairly near the ground. There the blackbird rears from three to six young ones. Development is very rapid. Incubation takes 13 or 14 days and after another 13 or 14 days of being fed by their parents, the young blackbirds can fly.

The crossbill is known as the gypsy among birds. It has no home and no regular habits. Sometimes, when the pine trees have produced a lot of seeds, the crossbill appears suddenly and invades the woods. The season doesn't matter — the invasion may come in December or in May. Crossbills make their nests, lay their eggs, raise their brood and go off again. No one knows where they came from or where they go. Many years may pass before they reappear.

The crossbill is somewhat larger than the sparrow. The male is bright red, the female is duller. The name comes from the fact that the two halves of the beak are crossed when closed.

Pine and fir seeds are their main food. Their nests, built high in the pine trees, are made of twigs and moss, lined with feathers.

Crossbill→

The nuthatch, a small bird with a long beak and short tail, is common in the woods. It chases insects and spiders on the tree trunks, and eats small nuts and various other seeds.

It nests in the holes of trees or walls. The nest consists of small flakes of bark (mostly pine) applied to the walls of the cavity so as to form a continuous covering. The nuthatch blocks the entrance to the hole by building a wall of clay, leaving only a narrow opening. The partition, dotted with peck-marks, can be seen in the photograph. In the opening you can barely see a young bird's gaping beak. Incubation lasts 13 or 14 days, and the young birds fly at the age of three weeks.

Nightingale

It is in May and June that the nightingale's song becomes most beautiful. This is the brooding period. The nightingale's nest is built on the ground or near the ground in a hedge. It is made of dry leaves, plant stalks and small roots, brought together and molded into a deep cup. It contains four or five glossy brown eggs.

The female nightingale sits on them for 12 to 14 days. The male feeds the female during the long hours she spends motionless on the nest. Both parents look after the young ones, who fly away when they are about 12 days old.

INDEX